SCIENCE ON THE
MAYFLOWER

by Tammy Enz

CAPSTONE PRESS
a capstone imprint

T0020372

Capstone Captivate is published by Capstone Press, an imprint of Capstone.
1710 Roe Crest Drive
North Mankato, Minnesota 56003
www.capstonepub.com

Library of Congress Cataloging-in-Publication Data is available on the Library of Congress website.
ISBN: 978-1-4966-9573-4 (library binding)
ISBN: 978-1-4966-9694-6 (paperback)
ISBN: 978-1-9771-5916-8 (eBook PDF)

Summary: You may have heard of the *Mayflower* and how the ship carried the Pilgrims across the sea. But did you know that science played a big role in their voyage? Learn how science helped the Pilgrims make the journey across the ocean and build a new home for themselves in the New World.

Editorial Credits
Editors, Angie Kaelberer and Aaron Sautter; Designer, Kazuko Collins; Media Researcher, Svetlana Zhurkin; Production Specialist, Kathy McColley

Image Credits
Alamy: Chronicle, 34, Science History Images, 22, The Bookworm Collection, 36; Architect of the Capitol: 4; Bridgeman Images: © Look and Learn, 15, 32, Peter Newark Pictures, 44; Capstone: 13, 25; Getty Images: Bettmann, cover (bottom), 1 (top), Interim Archives, 39; Library of Congress: 12, 40, 45; NASA: 27; Newscom: Heritage Images/Ann Ronan Picture Library, 16, Universal Images Group/De Agostini Picture Library, 14, World History Archive, 21; NOAA: 26; North Wind Picture Archives: 7, 9, 42; Shutterstock: Athawit Ketsak, 18, 19, Ethan Daniels, 24, Formatoriginal, 35, KamimiArt (design element), 1 (bottom) and throughout, Kateryna Kon, 33, Maryia Kazakova, 37, Nicku, 28, Nitr, 17 (right), 23, Peter Hermes Furian, 11, Rainer Lesniewski, cover (top), 31, StepanPopov, 17 (left), Suchan, 41, VectorMine, 20; Smithsonian American Art Museum: Gift of International Business Machines Corporation, 30; Wikimedia: Mushpot, 29; XNR Productions: 5

Printed and bound in China. 4205

TABLE OF CONTENTS

Words in **bold** text are included in the glossary.

CHAPTER 1

A NEW WORLD

In 1620, a small group of people known as Separatists were searching for something they couldn't find in Europe. They wanted a place to worship the way they wished. They didn't want to follow the Church of England. Some moved to the Netherlands, but they weren't happy there either.

The Pilgrims sailed for America in 1620 to start a new life and to seek religious freedom.

Journey of the *Mayflower*

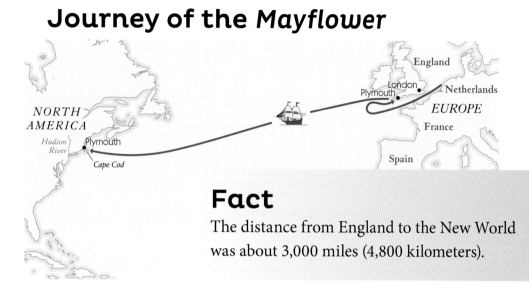

Fact

The distance from England to the New World was about 3,000 miles (4,800 kilometers).

Across the Atlantic Ocean was North America—a place the Europeans called the New World. In America, the Separatists could live freely. Forty Separatists who called themselves "Saints" decided to make the journey. They joined with a group of fellow travelers whom they called "Strangers." Together they would sail to this strange new place. The travelers would later become known as the Pilgrims.

The Pilgrims knew little about the New World or the hardships of being at sea for months. But they did know a little about science. Science guided their travels. They applied their knowledge of the tools needed to navigate their ship. They also relied on science to build a community and grow food in a new place. They used what they knew to survive a dangerous trip into uncharted territory.

CHANGE IN PLANS

The Pilgrims got permission to start a settlement near the mouth of the Hudson River in North America. This river flows through what is now the state of New York. They found a ship called the *Mayflower* to carry them to their new home.

In July 1620, the Pilgrims packed their supplies on the ship in Southampton, England. There they planned to meet the *Mayflower*'s sister ship, the *Speedwell*, and make the trip together.

But the *Speedwell* was in trouble. It was leaking badly. Twice in August, the Pilgrims started out but had to return to patch the *Speedwell*. They patched the leaks with tar, a sticky substance made from tree roots. Tar is used to make ships watertight. But it couldn't help the *Speedwell*. On September 6, 1620, the Pilgrims left the *Speedwell* behind and headed out on the *Mayflower*. The ship was packed tightly with the extra travelers from the *Speedwell*. The Pilgrims had been on the ship since late July. Supplies were already running low.

Some Pilgrims from the Netherlands first traveled onboard the *Speedwell* (left front) to meet up with the *Mayflower* in England.

Later, the Pilgrims learned that the *Speedwell*'s owner had caused the ship to leak on purpose. He didn't want to be part of the trip. He fitted the ship with a mast that was much too large. Like a giant pry bar, the heavy mast pulled apart the planks in the ship's hull.

Fact

The *Mayflower*'s final head count was 102 passengers and about 30 crew members.

CHAPTER 2

FIGHTING NATURE'S FORCES

The delays before setting sail meant more bad news for the Pilgrims. They would be sailing during the Atlantic storm season. It also meant battling the westerlies. These strong winds are caused by warm air moving from the **equator** toward the cold polar regions.

This warm air circulates. In the northern Atlantic Ocean, air currents push from the west. Westerlies are stronger in winter. The *Mayflower* sailed against these winds as it headed west.

The winds pushed on the *Mayflower*. When ships move through air and water, the air and water push back. This resisting force is called drag. Drag slows ships down.

It took the Pilgrims 66 days to sail to America. When the *Mayflower* returned to England in 1621, it took less than half that time. The westerly winds and ocean currents helped push it back to England.

To cross the Atlantic Ocean, the *Mayflower* had to battle through storms, headwinds, and ocean currents that flowed east instead of west.

BATTLING OCEAN CURRENTS

The *Mayflower* traveled only about 2 miles (3.2 km) per hour. The crew members knew they would be fighting the west winds as they sailed east. But they didn't know ocean currents would be pushing against them too.

In the 1600s, sailors didn't know about the Gulf Stream. This warm ocean current is located in the North Atlantic Ocean. Ocean currents are similar to rivers running through the ocean. They move water from warmer places to colder places. The area at the equator is warm all year. This is because the sun is directly overhead at the equator, rather than slanted as it is at the poles. Warm water near the equator flows toward the colder North and South Poles.

The warm Gulf Stream flows north from the Gulf of Mexico near the east coast of the United States. Then it heads east across the ocean to England. The Gulf Stream pushed against the *Mayflower*, slowing it even more.

The Gulf Stream

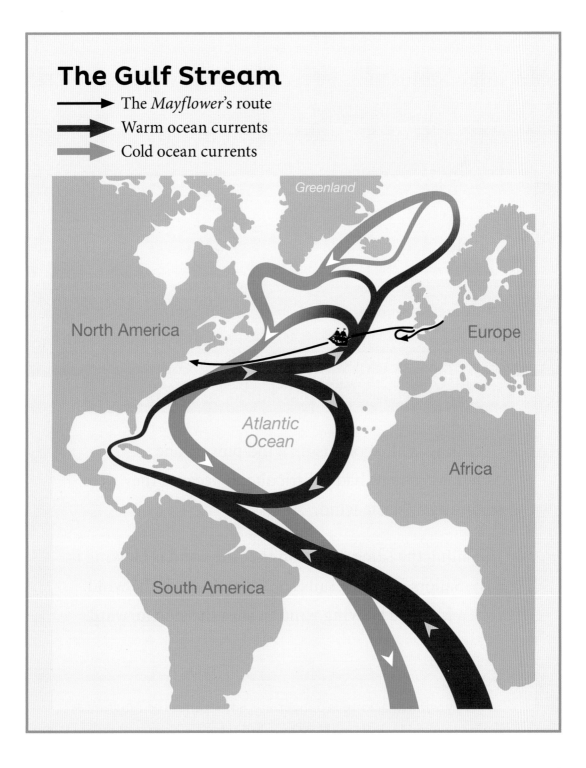

➤ The *Mayflower*'s route
➤ Warm ocean currents
➤ Cold ocean currents

Greenland

North America

Europe

Atlantic
Ocean

Africa

South America

11

If the wind was in the right direction, the *Mayflower* traveled quickly. But the crew often had to turn the sails from side to side to catch the wind. This caused the ship to travel much slower.

Sailing is all about using wind power. The *Mayflower*'s crew had a difficult job because they were sailing against the wind.

Sailing the same direction that the wind is blowing is easy. Sailors open the sails so that they catch the wind. Like a kite, the blowing wind pushes the ship forward.

Fact

In heavy winds, tacking is dangerous. Sometimes the *Mayflower* had to take up its sails and let the wind take it wherever it wanted.

But when the wind is blowing opposite to the ship's direction, the ship is sailing upwind. It's very tough to sail upwind. But the science of physics makes it possible. When sailing upwind, sailors turn the sails to catch the wind at an angle. The sails change the direction of the wind's force. The ship's **keel** balances some of the force. But the force also moves the ship forward and to one side. The sailors then change the angle of the sails so the wind pushes the ship forward to the other side. The ship slowly zigzags forward. This sailing method is called tacking.

Sailing Upwind: Tacking

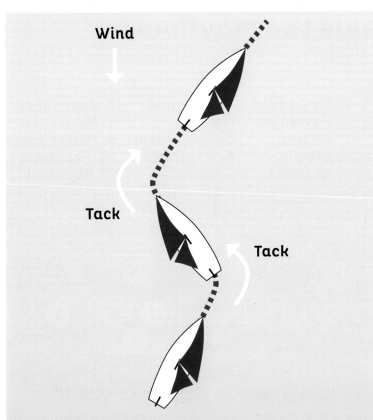

CHAPTER 3

LIFE ON THE MAYFLOWER

The first half of the Pilgrims' trip passed slowly. Then disaster struck. Fierce storms raged as the passengers huddled in their small living area on the *Mayflower*'s gun deck. The rocking of the ship left many too seasick to get out of bed.

Inside the *Mayflower*

1. Cargo hold
2. Passenger section
3. Crew's quarters
4. Steerage room
5. Tiller room
6. Captain's cabin
7. Upper deck
8. Main mast
9. Mizzen mast
10. Foremast
11. Bowsprit

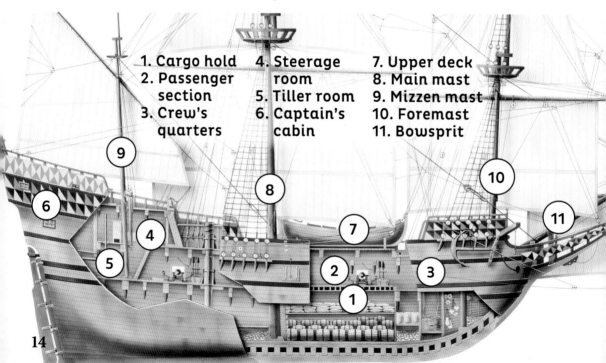

The Pilgrims often felt seasick as the *Mayflower* was tossed and rocked by fierce storms at sea.

Seasickness causes nausea, dizziness, and vomiting. But seasickness isn't related to a stomach illness. It is actually caused by an inner ear disturbance.

The inner ear contains a person's balance system. The body can feel a boat bobbing and swaying. But the eyes see only the unmoving inside of the cabin or the ship's deck. The brain doesn't know what to do with this imbalance. It sends out large amounts of stress **hormones** to deal with the issue. High levels of these hormones can cause nausea and vomiting.

At that time there was no treatment for seasickness other than to get used to it. Once people adjusted to the imbalance on the ship, the symptoms usually stopped.

PRESERVING FOOD SUPPLIES

The Pilgrims had to pack enough food to last for their entire journey and as they built their new colony. But the food had to be well-preserved to last a long time. Eating spoiled food can lead to food poisoning.

The Pilgrims took both fresh and preserved food on their journey. Any fresh food had to be eaten before it spoiled. Dried and salted foods could last for several months at sea.

Spoiled apples

Dried apples

Bacteria are the main cause of food spoilage. Bacteria are tiny organisms that are located almost everywhere, including in food. Over time, the bacteria break down the cells in food and cause it to spoil. Bacteria need warmth and moisture to do their work. The Pilgrims didn't have freezers to store their food. So their best bet was to dry it.

Fruits and vegetables can be dried in ovens or in the sun. The Pilgrims dried meat by rubbing it with salt or soaking it in salt water. The salt draws water out of the food cells to remove moisture.

Among the Pilgrims' most important supplies were their casks of beer. In the 1600s, people didn't have ways to treat drinking water. Germs in water often made it unsafe to drink. Beer was made through boiling and **fermenting** water and grain. This process created alcohol, which killed dangerous germs and made it safer to drink. Even young children drank beer.

CHAPTER 4

TOOLS OF THE TRADE

The Pilgrims packed more than food and beer in the ship's cargo section. They also brought many tools, including a **screw jack**. They may have brought this large tool to help them build homes in the New World. But the screw jack probably saved the *Mayflower* from being shipwrecked. Without it, the Pilgrims might not have made it to North America.

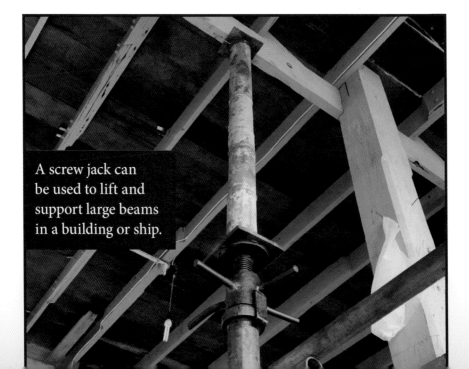

A screw jack can be used to lift and support large beams in a building or ship.

How a Screw Jack Works

Turning the handle moves the screw rod up or down through the threaded block. This movement helps raise or lower a heavy object.

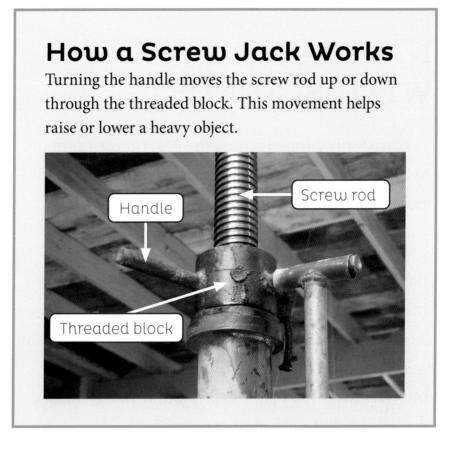

Handle

Screw rod

Threaded block

One especially violent storm cracked the ship's masts and shredded its sails. But even worse, it cracked the main support beam. The crew had a wooden post in the hold that could be used to support the cracked beam. But they first had to lift the broken beam back into place. That's where the screw jack came in handy. The crew members cranked the large screw jack to lift the heavy beam. Then they could place the post under it. Thanks to the screw jack, they saved the *Mayflower*.

NAVIGATING WITH SCIENCE

Christopher Jones Jr. was the *Mayflower*'s captain. As he charted the ship's course, Jones had only a few tools to help him.

Imaginary lines on Earth called latitude and longitude are used to locate places on Earth. Latitude lines are horizontal. They measure the distance between the equator and the North and South Poles. Longitude lines are vertical. They measure the distance east and west from the Prime Meridian, which is located in Greenwich, England. If travelers have a location's latitude and longitude, they can travel to it.

Latitude and Longitude

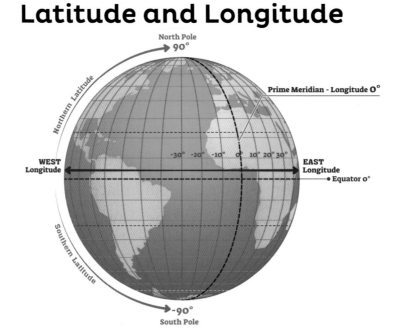

Magnetic Compass

Another navigational tool the *Mayflower*'s crew used was a compass. A compass is a magnetic device. Wherever you are on Earth, a compass needle always points north. A compass works because Earth's iron core makes it act like a giant magnet. It has a magnetic North Pole and a magnetic South Pole. Hikers, sailors, and even airplane pilots still use compasses today.

Captain Jones had no tools to find his longitude. But he could find his latitude using a cross-staff. This 3-foot (1-meter) stick with a slider measured the sun's angle from the horizon at midday. The sun moves north and south across the sky throughout the seasons. Knowing the date and the location of the sun from the horizon helped sailors pinpoint their latitude. They used the information to find their latitude in a nautical almanac. This book showed the position of the sun and stars. The *Mayflower* crew members learned that winds had pushed the ship much farther north than they had planned.

A ship's navigator could use a cross-staff and the sun's position to determine how far north or south the ship had traveled.

21

MEASURING SPEED

The *Mayflower*'s crew members knew that they were traveling slowly. Supplies were running low, and the passengers were getting restless.

To find the ship's speed, the crew used a log line. A log line is a rope with a weighted log attached to one end. The log floats on water. The log line's rope has knots tied every seven fathoms. One fathom is equal to 6 feet (1.8 m).

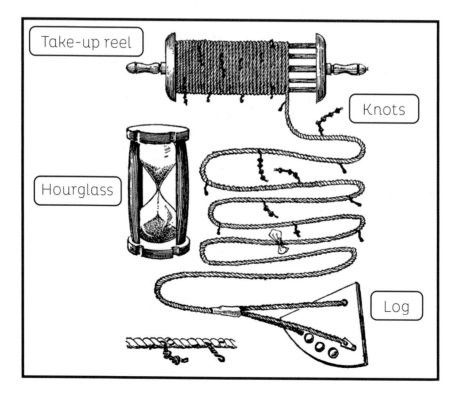

Take-up reel

Knots

Hourglass

Log

Keeping Time

The Pilgrims measured time with an hourglass. This device has two bulbs of glass, one on top of the other. It's filled with sand. It takes exactly one hour for the sand to pour through a narrow neck between the bulbs. It then is turned over to time the next hour. The Pilgrims likely also used smaller sandglasses to measure shorter periods of time, such as the 28 seconds used in counting knots.

The crew members wound the rope on a reel and tossed the log overboard. As the ship sailed away from the log, they counted the number of knots that passed over the ship's edge in 28 seconds. The number of knots gave them their speed. Ships still measure their speed in knots today.

Fact

A knot is one nautical mile per hour. It's equal to a land speed of 1.15 miles (1.85 km) per hour.

CHAPTER 5

NOWHERE TO LAND

After more than two months at sea, the Pilgrims saw seagulls in the sky. The birds meant that land was nearby. On November 9, 1620, they spotted land.

But they weren't at their planned landing site. The ship was 220 miles (354 km) north of the Hudson River, near Cape Cod in present-day Massachusetts. While the crew could see the trees near shore, they couldn't get to land. Barrier beaches blocked the ship's path.

Barrier beaches near Cape Cod, Massachusetts, make it nearly impossible for large ships to approach the main shoreline.

Riptide Formation

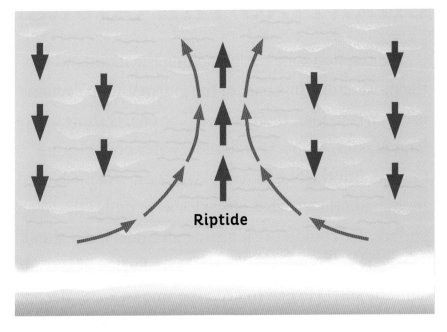

Riptide

A barrier beach is a long strip of land parallel to the mainland. It's formed by storms and **erosion**. Hidden shoals and deadly riptides surrounded the barrier beaches. Riptides occur when tides wash up on the shore. The barrier beaches block water from the ocean. The water rushes along the shore to a break in the beach. It then swirls through like in a draining sink. Sailing through a riptide could tear the ship apart.

When the *Mayflower* couldn't get to shore, the crew steered the ship south. They headed toward the Hudson River.

CHARTING THE COURSE

For Captain Jones, approaching the mainland was the most dangerous part of the journey. Ship captains use charts to plan their routes. The charts show where land masses, harbors, and underwater obstacles are located. But the North American coast was uncharted. Jones had no idea what obstacles were under the water's surface. He couldn't risk hitting an underwater shoal and tearing a hole in the cargo hold. Such a hole could sink the ship. He had to keep the ship in water deep enough to avoid such damage.

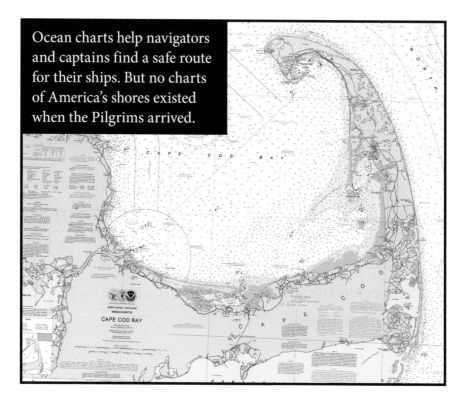

Ocean charts help navigators and captains find a safe route for their ships. But no charts of America's shores existed when the Pilgrims arrived.

The crew used sounding lines to check the water's depth. This device was a rope with a lead weight on one end. The rope was marked at each fathom. Sailors dropped the device into the ocean. When the lead weight sank to the ocean bottom, crew members read the depth in fathoms off the rope.

Dangerous Shoals

Shoals are ridges of sand or gravel below the water's surface that create an area of shallow water. They can be dangerous to ships. Their depth can vary depending on the tides. Tides are the daily rising and falling of ocean water. They're caused by the moon's gravity pulling on Earth. An area that is safe at one time might be dangerous later when the tide goes out.

Cape Cod and dangerous shoals (lower right) as seen from space.

STEERING TO SHORE

The crew's helmsman steered the ship using a rudder. This small flap is at the back of the ship beneath the water. The helmsman directed the rudder from above in an area called the steerage room. He used a long pole called a whipstaff. It was attached to a handle on the rudder called a tiller through a hole in the hull.

Scientist Isaac Newton's third law of motion says that for every action, there is an equal and opposite reaction. So pushing the rudder in one direction causes a ship to move in the opposite direction.

Newton's Laws of Motion

In the late 1600s, Sir Isaac Newton discovered three laws that describe how things move.

1. An object at rest will stay at rest and a moving object will keep moving unless acted on by an outside force.

2. A force is equal to an object's mass multiplied by its acceleration.

3. For every action, there is an equal and opposite reaction.

Sir Isaac Newton

The helmsman's job was especially important when steering along the hidden shoals. He could see neither the rudder nor the direction the boat was headed. He had to blindly follow the captain's directions. He had to make quick, exact movements to keep the ship from hitting the rocky shoals.

Steering the *Mayflower*

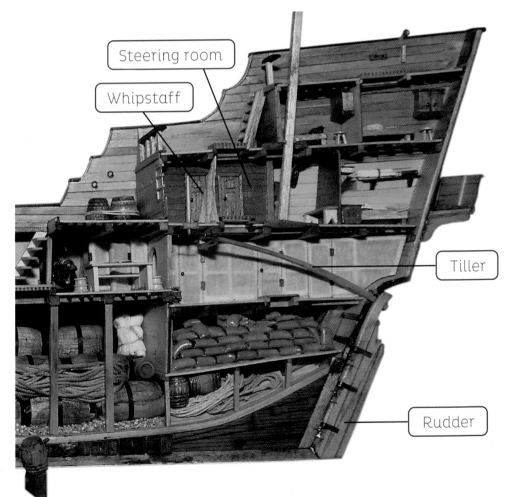

Steering room

Whipstaff

Tiller

Rudder

WINTER SHELTER

One day after the *Mayflower* headed south, the wind's direction changed. It became a headwind that blew against the ship. Captain Jones feared the strong headwind would push the ship into the rocky coast if they continued south. The Pilgrims decided to head back to Cape Cod to spend the winter and look for a place to settle.

Fact

While docked in the harbor, the Pilgrims wrote a set of rules called the Mayflower Compact to govern their new settlement. Forty-one of the men aboard the ship signed the compact. At the time, women had few legal rights and weren't allowed to sign the document.

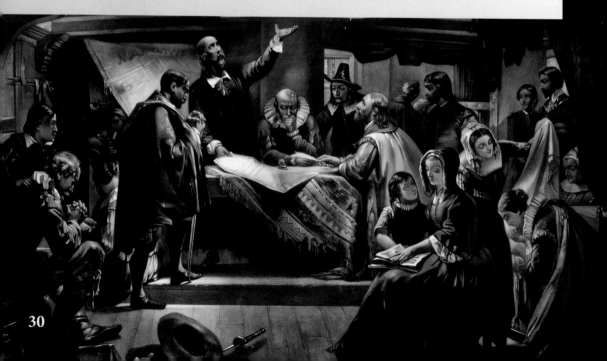

The *Mayflower*'s Journey to Cape Cod

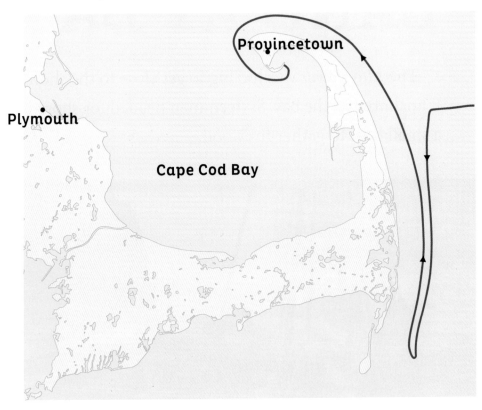

On November 11, 1620, the *Mayflower* sailed into what is now Provincetown Harbor in Massachusetts. The Pilgrims had struggled through seasickness, storms, and a damaged ship for more than two months at sea. But they had finally arrived at the New World.

CHAPTER 6

LAND AT LAST

The *Mayflower* was too big to get close to the shore. It anchored in the bay. Sixteen men headed for shore in a small boat to gather firewood.

After reaching Cape Cod, colony leader Myles Standish led a small group of men to explore and search for a suitable place for the Pilgrims to land.

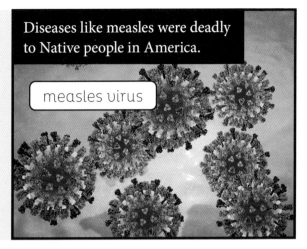

Diseases like measles were deadly to Native people in America.

measles virus

The men expected to see Native people on shore. The area was home to the Wampanoag people. But they found no one. Science explains why. Earlier European explorers had brought deadly diseases with them. The body's immune system keeps people safe from disease. When people are exposed to a virus or bacteria, they develop **antibodies** to fight the disease. These antibodies stay with the person. When later exposed to a similar virus or bacteria, the immune system recognizes the invader. It quickly makes the white blood cells needed to fight the disease.

But the Wampanoag and other Native people had never been exposed to European diseases. They had no immunity to fight the illnesses. Many died from the diseases that Europeans could survive.

TOXIC TREATS

The Pilgrims planned to spend the winter on the ship. But they needed to find a place on land to build their settlement after winter was over. Those who explored the shores were happy to find sea creatures called mussels. It was their first fresh food in a long time.

After several months at sea, the Pilgrims were eager to go ashore to wash clothes and find fresh food.

wild mussels

The Pilgrims eagerly ate the seafood, but it only added to their problems. Many suffered from sudden diarrhea and vomiting. Mussels are filter feeders. As they move through the water, they pump water into their bodies. They then filter the water, pulling out bits of organic matter for food. They then pump the water out of their bodies.

The Pilgrims didn't know that mussels sometimes eat algae containing **toxins**. The toxins stay in the mussels, and cooking doesn't remove them. The toxins don't have a taste or smell, but they can poison people who eat them.

A NEW CROP

As a group of Pilgrims searched for a place to build, they found Native villages that had been abandoned. They also discovered graves. They then came across a site where the soil had been dug up, replaced, and smoothed over. The men wondered what could be buried there.

Fact

Corn is one of the world's most important crops. More than 1.1 billion tons are grown each year.

The corn we know today was first developed in Mexico. People crossed a tall, broad-leaf grass called teosinte with other plants to create the first corn plants.

They began digging. What they found wasn't gold. But to the starving Pilgrims, it was even better. They found corn. Corn was new to the Europeans, but the Wampanoag and other people had been planting and eating it for thousands of years. They created a **hybrid** plant by crossing two plants with different traits. The pollen from one plant's tassel is combined with the silk of another plant to create hybrid kernels of grain. Over many years, people continued this process to produce corn with large, edible kernels. People still use this process to make improved varieties of corn.

Cross-Pollination

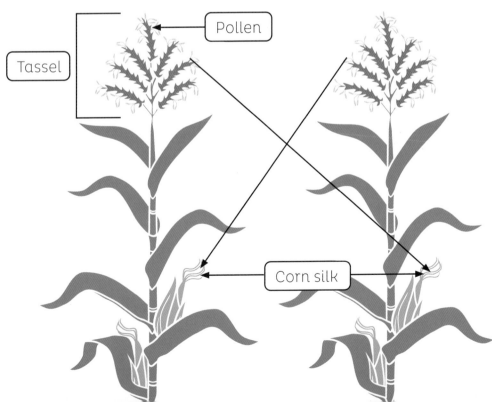

Tassel

Pollen

Corn silk

A BITTER WINTER

The Pilgrims knew they would arrive in the New World in late fall. But they weren't prepared for the cold weather. Cape Cod is farther south than England, so the Pilgrims expected it to be warmer. But it wasn't.

Weather on the U.S. east coast mostly moves across land from the west. Land cools much faster than water. So Cape Cod usually has cold winters. Weather patterns in England also come from the west. But they begin in the Atlantic Ocean. Water stays warm longer than land. This helps create warmer weather in winter. The reverse is true in the summer.

North America was also affected at that time by a weather pattern called the "Little Ice Age." In the late 1200s, several large volcanic eruptions threw huge amounts of ash into the atmosphere. This ash cloud blocked some of the sun's rays, causing Earth's temperature to cool. The cooling trend lasted for several hundred years.

The Pilgrims were used to mild winters in England. They weren't prepared for the cold weather they experienced during their first winter in the New World.

CHAPTER 7

BUILDING A NEW COLONY

The Pilgrims had no luck finding a proper place to build a settlement. As they searched, they found more deserted villages. Nothing felt right about this new place.

The *Mayflower* finally arrived at Plymouth Harbor on December 16, 1620.

Plymouth Rock

Stories about the Pilgrims' landing at Plymouth Harbor include a large boulder in the harbor. While this rock did exist, stories about the Pilgrims using it to step off the ship onto land were first told more than 100 years later. No one is sure if the story is true or a legend. Over the years, Plymouth Rock has been moved, broken in two, and chipped into pieces. The rock was cemented together and now rests back in Plymouth Harbor.

The *Mayflower* then headed north about 34.5 miles (55.6 km) and anchored in Plymouth Harbor. A few days later, the Pilgrims chose a new place for a permanent settlement. The area had freshwater springs. Freshwater was the Pilgrims' most important need. People can't drink salty ocean water. Human body cells are made mostly from water. Salt pulls water out of the cells. Without water, body cells die. **Dehydration** can be fatal.

The Pilgrims chose to settle at the site of a former Pawtuxet nation village. Most of the Native people there had died from diseases or war. Their bones were still scattered around the site.

DISEASE AND DEATH

Only one Pilgrim, William Butten, had died during the journey to the New World. But the worst was yet to come. Disease often spreads rapidly when people are living close together. **Pneumonia** and **tuberculosis** infected many people on the ship during the Pilgrims' first winter in Plymouth Harbor. These diseases can be deadly. Today both diseases are treated with antibiotics, which weren't discovered until the 1920s.

After landing at Plymouth, the Pilgrims soon began building a large common house using trees and other materials they found in the area.

Fact

Although disease sickened many of the Pilgrims onboard the *Mayflower*, the settlers still had to build their new settlement. They built a 400-square-foot (37-square-m) building called a common house. They built walls from tree trunks woven together with branches and cemented together with clay. The roof was thatched with reeds. This wattle-and-daub construction was similar to country English homes.

As they built, the Pilgrims glimpsed Native people watching. On March 16, a tall Native man strolled into the settlement. He greeted the settlers by saying, "Welcome, Englishmen!" The man's name was Samoset. He was part of a nearby group of Wampanoag people. He said he learned to speak a little English from fishermen who had visited the area earlier. He said another Native man in the area, Squanto, spoke even better English than he did.

HELPFUL NEIGHBORS

By spring, the *Mayflower* headed back to England. The Pilgrims now had to make it on their own. But Squanto provided a lot of help. He helped the Pilgrims form a peace treaty with the local Native nations.

The Native people helped the Pilgrims learn how to farm and hunt. The New England soil was of poor quality. The Native people showed the Pilgrims how to fertilize their crops. They placed a small fish in each hole as they planted seeds. When the fish decayed, it released nutrients into the soil. The plants pulled the nutrients in through their roots. This helped the plants grow strong and produce a lot of food.

Squanto and other Native people taught the Pilgrims how to grow their own food in the poor New England soil.

The First Thanksgiving

At harvest time after their first summer in the New World, the Pilgrims held a great feast. For three days they celebrated and gave thanks to God and their Native friends for a good harvest. About 90 Native people,  including Squanto, joined in the celebration.

Today many Native nations view Thanksgiving as a day of mourning. They feel that the holiday marks the beginning of the end of their way of life. The Wampanoag people and the Pilgrims were friendly toward one another. But thousands of Native people were later hurt or killed by other European settlers.

After a summer of building homes and planting and storing food, the Pilgrims were ready for winter. They had used science to travel to the New World. And science helped them build a new home. Their successes and failures laid the foundation for the growth of a new nation.

GLOSSARY

antibody (AN-ti-bah-dee)—a substance produced by the white blood cells that fights infection and disease

dehydration (dee-hy-DRAY-shuhn)—a life-threatening medical condition caused by lack of water

erosion (i-ROH-zhuhn)—wearing away of rock or soil by wind, water, or ice

equator (i-KWAY-tur)—an imaginary line around Earth's middle, halfway between the North and South Poles

fermentation (fur-men-TAY-shuhn)—a chemical reaction by microbes such as yeast and bacteria that causes changes in food

hormone (HOR-mohn)—a chemical made by a gland that affects growth and body processes

hybrid (HYE-brid)—a plant or animal bred from two different species or varieties

keel (KEEL)—a long beam along the bottom of a ship that holds the ship together

pneumonia (noo-MOH-nyuh)—a serious disease that causes the lungs to become inflamed and filled with a thick liquid that makes breathing difficult

screw jack (SKROO JAK)—a screw-operated jack used for lifting, exerting pressure, or adjusting the position of an object

toxin (TOK-sin)—a poisonous substance produced by a living thing

tuberculosis (tu-bur-kyuh-LOH-siss)—a serious bacterial disease that causes fever, weight loss, coughing, and difficulty breathing

READ MORE

Byers, Ann. *Squanto.* New York: Cavendish Square, 2021.

Rusick, Jessica. *Sailing on the Mayflower: A This or That Debate.* North Mankato, MN: Capstone Press, 2020.

Son, John. *If You Were a Kid on the Mayflower.* New York: Children's Press, 2018.

Yolen, Jane. *Plymouth Rocks!: The Stone-Cold Truth.* Watertown, MA: Charlesbridge, 2020.

INTERNET SITES

Colonial America: Mayflower
www.ducksters.com/history/colonial_america/mayflower.php

The First Thanksgiving
www.scholastic.com/scholastic_thanksgiving/voyage/

Mayflower Facts for Kids
kids.kiddle.co/Mayflower

INDEX